EUPHONIOUS NATURA

A collection of poems

JERLIN FLOWER S

Preface

"Adopt the pace of nature,

Her secret is patience"

-*Ralph Waldo Emerson*

As poet Emerson said, nature is peaceful. Nature has intense Patience and has solutions to every issue. Nothing can exist without nature. Without bargaining, nature bestows its generosity and affection to all. In this book, "Euphonious Natura" the author expresses her love and passion fornature and how nature gave her Solutions.

Also, this book brings about the worth of music. Music is a form of nature, comforting and soothing broken hearts. Music is a healer, a refreshment for tired souls!

"Music is the mediator between

the spiritual and the sensual life"

-Beethoven

Beethoven said, Music is a pathway. Our author has journeyed through it and has inked the notesof music in lyrical poems of deep significance and greatness.

Enjoy reading the book, "Euphonious Natura" which will fascinate the readers and immerse them in the beauty of music and elegance of nature!

NATURE- THE RELIEVER

With a cup of coffee,
I closed my eyes,
Heeded to the music,
Raindrops gave me a rhythm to sing.

I walked, strode,
Through the grasses,
Explored the beauty,
And enjoyed the moisture in it.

The swords of grass slashed,
Felt a rush in me,
Stepped of it, crouched down, and saw,
The beauty of the earth in yellow flowers.

A pink structure caught my eyes,
Along with the muddy trench of dirty water.
Nearing, Lotus it is!
Beauty amongst the unpleasant earth.

The incarnation of happiness,
In lotus and yellow flower,
Made up for the slashed ache.
Depicting, nature relieving anguish!!!

TEARS OF TWILIGHT

Twilight of darkness,
Gave me a stab,
The stab of a betrayer,
Without a knife – but
With the sword of words.

Wounding my heart,
Would leave a scar, but
You shuddered the soul of mine.
Sword of words stabbed,
My soul, My soul!!

The tears developed
Into the tears of ocean.
Silence of him became mine,
Not in joy -but
In fierce grief.

My trust became,
Broken trust.
My Heart became a broken heart.
You broke it,
Not mine, it's yours!!!!

THE NATURE'S CREATOR

The creator refreshed,
Refreshed everyone, everywhere to be replenished.
Sculpted everyone to be loved
Made myself to be loved.

You never got tired
Of listening, of emotions,
The tears in me are wiped
And the desire of my heart, fulfilled.

You held me with a joy of my heart,
Gifted me the art of heaven.
Made every day a sunny day,
To shine like the sun.

Made every human - feel the agony,
And feel the agony of others.
Music in me evolved,
To sing, sing, sing only for you.

ALONE IN DARK

It was a gloomy night,
She sat on the stairs,
Looking at the stars,
She loves, loved
Being in darkness.

She enjoyed the beauty of the night,
She loved darkness than the light,
As she tasted life's darkness.
And found her courage in loneliness.

Looking at the moonlight,
 Wanting to bring needy to light.
To make them feel 'good night'.
She bid goodbye.

Acknowledgment

"Soli Deo Gloria" (To God alone be the Glory), My first and foremost gratitude is to God Almighty, who helped me throughout writing this book and still keeps on aiding me on the trackof achievements. I would like to thank my beloved uncle **Rosian. N**, a noble and good- hearted man, for supporting me in my writing journey. I want to thank my Head of the Department Prof.**J.Robinson** and my lovely friend **Anne Benita.D** for their constant assistance and encouragement. I also want to thank my dear students **Riya Richard.R.L** and **Aathisha John Kennady** and **Lisa J Silva** for their affection and support. Last but not least, I'm thankful to all my friends, family members, colleagues and my students for their love and motivation towards me.

This is my third solo book. Being a lover of nature and music, I have written this book, "Euphonious Natura" - a collection of musical and nature poems. Do enjoy reading and I can guarantee that you'll immerse in the rhythm of nature!

TABLE OF CONTENTS

THE HEART OF NATURE

The sweet tweet of birds,
The chillness of the early skies,
Wake me up in the mornings;

I fly to the green fields,
Along with other flies,
Buzzing like the busy bees;

The fresh scent of grasses,
Dance of fishes and prawns,
Bring me to play in the streams;

Catching the stinging catfishes,
Along with my troops,
Makes me feel togetherness;

When I set out into the Nature,
My heart is filled with merry,
Because of the heart of nature;

Which delights my soul,
Making me forget all the pain,
By its pleasant sparkling beauty!

MY HOMELAND

It's hot!!! Very hot here...
The summer made me unhealthy,
With rashes, fever, and headache;

Every day was an irritation,
My soul longed for my homeland!
"My Homeland"- the harmonic land!

Every dawn and dusk ...
Your chill made my soul energized;
You gave extraneous power everyday...

Your every season is rainy,
Every sunset makes me
Ease up my painful heart,

With new hope and strength,
I open my eyes every day
Under the warm shadow of yours

Now, we're both apart but
The cloudy skies, and the breeze here,Makes me feel you
at my heart!

THE RHYTHM OF NATURE

An amazing journey with music
Gives a joyful soul to the universe,
Strong wings to the mind,
Flight to the imagination.

I wake up to the birds chirping
It cheers my heart, making my soul sing,
And gives thoughts a multi-splendored wing
They sing in unison
As though celebrating a special occasion
I add silence to their chorus-in between. . .

The rivers don't talk,
They just roll by. . .
Whispering to my soul,
To listen to the river,
That flows within me!

I breathe the aroma- the freshness,
I adore the greenery
The swaying of grass, rustling of leaves
As wind gushes through the trees
It's the Rhythm of nature-
The Mother Rhythm of music.

THE MEMORIES OF GREEN

The chirping of birds greeted me. . .
To feel the music in trees.
Cherries, custard apples,
Berries, water apples around
Made me feel the sweetness in my heart.

The beautiful roses made me
Wonder the beauty of art,
The smiling pansies made me
Smile deeply from my heart,
The white daisies made me
Realize the goodness of nature,

A real sweet home it is,
Tall trees and blue lakes
Happiness and joyfulness,
Replenished my mind
 The real bond of love.
As nature will never hurt
By its tender greens

Opened my eyes, it was not a dream
It's the memories of green!

GLISTER OF LIGHTNING

Raindrops greeted me-with
the beats of peaceful music,
The winds billowed me - with
A cool and sweet harmony

The silence of the notes;
Alleviated my mind to the sky
The thunder gave a roar
A signal of arrival...

For him, the lightning
He flashed in the sky
Like dividing the earth,
With a glister – said

"Be a glister"...
I was fascinated,
Realized and turned
Myself into a glister,
Shining like a glitter,
Making my life
Radiant and powerful!

THE DIVINE DUSK

On a chill divine dusk,

With the gloomy sky, dark clouds...

Walking on the streets

Talking with her heart,

Her heart beat is like

 The beats of raindrops

Her lips smiled and in wonder

The sky poured rain...

The rhythm of falling rain

Made her clutch the umbrella

Drops fell on her cheeks,

The windy breeze made her shiver,

Yet desired ice cream.

The taste of raindrops,

The dullness of the dusk sky

Gave delicious flavour of sweetness

THE LESSON OF CLOUDS

Clouds came floating,
She felt of dancing,
Like the clouds floating
To meet the trees?

The puzzles of her mind
They always float high
Refusing to carry burdens,
Or to paint the sky of the sunset.

The darkening clouds,
Showing the beauty of mountain,
And the art of buildings
Showing her the new path of river

She was amused,
As the clouds comforted her,
The clouds spoke to her,
She remained in deep silence

"Dear soul, be comforted to find the light,
The greater your storm,
The brighter your rainbow
Create your rainbow everyday!"

The clouds passed away
The lesson of the clouds,
Made her to move on
and create a radiant life!

REX OF THE BLESSED ROSE

The fragrance tender
With sweetness fills the air,
Showing the beauty from its root,
Reminding the remarkable woman of virtue,
Named him, the king of flowers.

The thorny stems of you is a strength.
Even if others are pierced,
You spread fragrance,
Bringing happiness being the Blessed.

Attracting everyone with yours fragrance,
Moulding your kingdom,
Not just with the name of the crown - but
With your hard work and efforts,
You are the real Rex !!!

THE OATH OF THE OCEAN

Listening to the rhythm,
Of the deep sea.
She closed her eyes...
Tears rolling down to its music.
Falling onto the shore sands.

Remembering the promise,
Of a stormy heart,
She fell and felt being,
On a separate island.
Away from the hunting world.

The ocean stirs her heart,
Inspiring it with imagination,
And bringing eternal joy,
To her soul, calming her mind,
And eliciting her spirit to fly.

Feeling the rhythm of the sea,
The waves comforted her to aspire again...
Hugging her in the deep blue sea.
Inspiring her to resemble it.
And to exhibit her beautiful smile !!!

Being broken by a fake oath,
The ocean gave her hope
a promising oath for her
Swearing to be with her,

Support and sustain her
Till the ocean waves rest,
For eternity... the oath
Made her travel with the waves!

THE GENUINE GARDENER

The gardener gloomed,
In tears and pain.
As he remembered
His Tri-Azalea.
As a bud, he watered,
Safeguarded them each and every day,
With care and security.
Being the sole reason to flourish...

The gardener desired
To unravel their fragrance
But... he preserved the flowers,
And crushed them,
To give the perfect,
Perfume of eternity.

He formulated Tri-Azalea
To compete with "Deca-Hydrangea!"
Providing each one, with a unique fragrance,
And taught them to live independently.
Being the greatest teacher!!!

HUGGING THE NATURE

The chill breeze filled
My soul and my heart
Of your presence
The excitement made me
A fairy...

The tweets of musical birds
The raindrops on daisies
The pleasing smell of coffee
Wrapped me holding you

The lovely trees and woods
Showed its beauty
Of the union we had
The miles of journey
Became ours, the endless one

The tune of nature
Made you gift me
A beautiful creation,
Of the heavenly art.

The leaves flew on the wind,
Reminding me the season autumn-but
The nodding trees showed me,
Its roots grip like my bond.

You held my hand tight
And moved for the miles
To our destination-and
To escape from reality.

I enjoyed...
Listening to you...
To have yours as mine...
You fulfilled my desire
As you're mine, I'm yours!!!

FAIRYTALE OF RED ROSES

Today was a fairytale,
Being around red roses,
Refreshed my true love for you.
Holding me in my happiness and sorrow.

The melodies of my heart,
Rejoiced at the look of your eyes.
My heart fluttered with seconds ticking,
At the mere thought of you, being near.

Each day passed by,
With your sweetheart by my side.
Hugging my soft soft teddy bear,
Made me fall in your trap filled with red red roses.

The love for music in me
Made me listen, listen to your harmonious voice.
And felt the rhythm of your heart,
Made it a piece of beautiful romantic music.

The heavenly feel of my soul
Made my heart smile...
But with the ocean of tears,
I woke to the painful reality of life.

REMINDED BY BIRDS

The colourful birds
Reminded me of the colourful memories,
Of travel and the joys
We had together.

The journey with you,
Made me comfortable,
And got rid of,
The painful reality.

The joy of your presence
Added days and years to my existence.
Yet, you left me as a guest,
A chief guest in reality!!!

THE RUBBER MILK

In the dark of midnight,
I saw candlelight,
And a scraping noise
I was puzzled,
Puzzled till the morning.
I woke up,
To know the reality
Found the oozing liquids
From the rubber trees
To the tiny little containers like Coconut shells.
The process in it,
The pain in it,
The smell in it,
Makes it a perfect eraser.
Showing us how to erase,
To wipe out the pain
Of others.

PEACEFUL TWILIGHT

The darkness took over slowly,

Bidding bye to twilight.

My mind filled with darkness,

It tore my heart.

Thinking the way, I was cheated,

By others and society.

And the thief of my thoughts,

The greater tension of mine,

Showed me, my potential

Stood up to be strong.

To reach my goal

By kicking of the thief of my thoughts!!!

THE PURE COCONUT

The wind that blows

Showed me the fingers

The fingers in a leaf

To sing for a rhythm

To remind the nature,

Who arranges to make

A perfect singing

like a pure coconut

Being hard in strictness

But sweet and soft

On the inside

A pure soul!

With taste of love

Deep, deep, inside!

WHAT IS MANGO?

The ripe summer mango
It is a song,
It is a season,
It's hot summer.

Living in the sunshine,
That powered gold
In the hillside.

But I hate being
In the yellow coloured season.
And yet loved to eat,
The yellow coloured fruit
When I just say, "Mango"
I mean "Man Go".

NATURE- THE RELIEVER

With a cup of coffee,
I closed my eyes,
Heeded to the music,
Raindrops gave me a rhythm to sing.

I walked, strode,
Through the grasses,
Explored the beauty,
And enjoyed the moisture in it.

The swords of grass slashed,
Felt a rush in me,
Stepped of it, crouched down, and saw,
The beauty of the earth in yellow flowers.

A pink structure caught my eyes,
Along with the muddy trench of dirty water.
Nearing, Lotus it is!
Beauty amongst the unpleasant earth.

The incarnation of happiness,
In lotus and yellow flower,
Made up for the slashed ache.
Depicting, nature relieving anguish!!!

TEARS OF TWILIGHT

Twilight of darkness,
Gave me a stab,
The stab of a betrayer,
Without a knife – but
With the sword of words.

Wounding my heart,
Would leave a scar, but
You shuddered the soul of mine.
Sword of words stabbed,
My soul, My soul!!

The tears developed
Into the tears of ocean.
Silence of him became mine,
Not in joy -but
In fierce grief.

My trust became,
Broken trust.
My Heart became a broken heart.
You broke it,
Not mine, it's yours!!!!

THE NATURE'S CREATOR

The creator refreshed,
Refreshed everyone, everywhere to be replenished.
Sculpted everyone to be loved
Made myself to be loved.

You never got tired
Of listening, of emotions,
The tears in me are wiped
And the desire of my heart, fulfilled.

You held me with a joy of my heart,
Gifted me the art of heaven.
Made every day a sunny day,
To shine like the sun.

Made every human - feel the agony,
And feel the agony of others.
Music in me evolved,
To sing, sing, sing only for you.

ALONE IN DARK

It was a gloomy night,
She sat on the stairs,
Looking at the stars,
She loves, loved
Being in darkness.

She enjoyed the beauty of the night,
She loved darkness than the light,
As she tasted life's darkness.
And found her courage in loneliness.

Looking at the moonlight,
 Wanting to bring needy to light.
To make them feel 'good night'.
She bid goodbye.

THE TWO LOVELY DOVES

Two doves freed their wings
Drifted up to the sky
Without a noise
They travelled together
To the ends of the sky.

The wings of one
Gave me the love,
Not, the hatred.
Gave me the peace,
Not, the violence.

I felt the peace of mind
In my heart.
Remembering the verse,
Leaving me with a gift,
Your peace of mind and heart!

HAPPINESS OF GARDEN

I wandered,
As the silent wind, kissed me.
I glanced
At the tiny cute Chikoo.

I fluttered
At the aroma of Custard Apple.
I carved
For the mouth watering, Jackfruit.

I raced
Behind squirrels,
Which gifted me, mangoes
Their sweetness exploring my sweet buds.

I walked,
To see an excellent soul,
Who was lying down.
Under a tree napping.

I stepped,
Near to my daddy, smiling,
And sharing our happiness,
Gazing at our garden

THE COOL RAIN DROPS

A cool crystal fell on my cheek,
Fell on my hands,
I closed my eyes
Relished the chill blowing softly,
The chill made my heart cold.
I felt your hands holding mine.
I listened to the sweet strings in my heart.
Of your presence
I smiled at you,
Of being with you.
The taste of the chocolate with crystals,
Made me feel,
The taste of you,
As being the sweetest,
Among all humans.
I held your hand tight,
To make my choice right
And I realized...
You are my dream!!!

THE TASTE OF BITTERGOURD

I loathed bitterness,
As a sweety was I, brought up,
In this world of bitterness.

Honey being my fondness,
The sweetest folk encircles me,
Feeling the sweetness of earth.

Growing up, losing relationships,
Heart ached, tears rolled,
Of knowing the bitter truth.

The taste of bitter gourd,
Resting in my taste buds
Bring back bitter memories.

Being with bitter people,
Evolved me into a bitter gourd.
The bitter became her better!!!

THE UNIQUE FRAGRANCE

Watching the perfect end

Of my day

Feeling the magic

Of tantalizing rays

Your unique fragrance

Called me.

To look at the beauty

As the wind blew,

Reminded me,

The love of you.

For my name

To be a unique fragrance.

SYMBOL OF SMILE

The glittering sun smiles,
With its golden gleam.
I closed my eyes to feel
The love of my heart,
As I recalled the promise of a smile.

Even in sadness
As my little one irritated,
A cry of anger made,
A beautiful smile came,
After ocean of tears!

The symbol of my glee,
Brought in my friendship.
Yet, smiled to
Irritate the haters,
Made them feel guilty!!!

I listened to the music,
As it made me smile
And to be an expert,
At hiding my grief,
Yes, I smile through my pain...

MY STORYTELLER

The chill breeze blew,
The rain droplets on my veggies,
Exhibit the beauty of nature.

Tasted the greenery
Every morning around me,
Around my little ones.

The beautiful art of tiny hands,
And the cool breeze,
Brought me to the miracle of God,

As on my child's birth,
Every morning, everyone said to me,
"He is weak and would have the defects".

I felt the blessings of God in me,
Through his awesome talents...
And talents of mine.

The curiosity in him
Made me laugh, yet
Forging me a curious mind for learning!!!

I call him a storyteller,
But, everyone calls me,
A storyteller!!!

THE POWER OF MUSIC

Being born as a queen with love richness,

Had a smiling face, healing

The pain and grief of many...

The warm kindness in her

Made everyone be with her.

The Power of music in her,

Made her be tuneful...

Even in distress times...

 Even in great happiness...

The music gave her life

Her loneliness turned music

Her only companion to depend on,

She holds onto her musical melody,

Which enlightened her with

Great power to reach the

Highest pitch despite barriers!

THE STRINGS OF SOUL

The strings of a guitar
Gave me a tune,
On self-expression
Of my little heart.

The Melody won,
The heart of my heart.
Even thwarting autism,
With pure compassion.

Clenching my heart,
My happiness was heard
On the strings,
Of the heavenly harp

As his heartstrings like,
A teddy, as he is,
Made me fall for
The soft, soft teddy.

THE STORY OF MUSIC

A pain, a huge pain!
Aches me, that tore my heart,
Into an inferno of grief.
Even as my eyes are closed,
My agony is unclosed!

Dreams were scattered,
Yet, I live an imaginary life.
 A sweet melody comforts me,
With a tune of melancholy
In the life of imagination.

The incurable ache,
Cured as I listened
To the strings of music,
And learned by it that,
Life becomes a story of music!

THE MUSICAL INSPIRATION

The music in me started

With the word 'Do',

Doing all of my heart's needs.

Obsession of mine,

Comforted me with

The notes of music.

To 'Re'consruct the life of 'Me',

To reach 'Fa'r away...

Into the wilderness of happiness.

Finding the 'So'lution of life,

Making others happy,

In 'La'rge number.

My heart rejoiced

With rolling 'Te'ars

To 'Do' more!!!

I was blank,

To erase my blankness,

I filled my paper

With emotions of my soul,

And breathing my heart.

Shed out my insecurities,

Reflected myself in the paper.

And burned out my thoughts,

It revealed my imperfections.

And Yes, I cherished my every flaw.

The paper became a mirror,

To see myself,

It pushed me into the brightness.

To get closer and closer to the stars.

And to fulfil every wish of my heart.

SANE MIND

A pain, immense pain

In my heart, it aches

As it tore my heart.

My agony is unclosed,

As my eyes are closed.

The dreams are scattered

But living in my dreams,

Is a sweet melody of comfort.

And a tune of melancholy,

In my present life of pain.

The incurable ache inspired me,

To listen to the strings of music,

And lean onto it for solace,

As life became

A miserable one to live.

LOVE OF PEN

As I held my pen,

I closed my eyes,

Tears rolled down my cheeks,

Recalling the beautiful memories,

I had lived.

Emotions sprinkled down,

Upon the white paper,

To inscribe the tongue,

And the words of my heart.

Into the musical notes, I carved.

A sweet melody gave me a soul,

To give a pen of love-and

A pen of friendship,

Not to erase off my memories-but

To wipe, grief out!

The ache... gave me a courage

To pen down the happiest things,

To give others

The happiness of the pen.

I write everything,

With My Parker love,

I adore it,

I live it...

JACK - MY LOVE

Dear Jack, my dear Love,
You're the king ,indeed...
You're born with a crown –
Without being crowned of gold,
You fulfill each one's desire,
You replenish the craving.

The little, numerous thorns in you
Gave me the realizations
The hard Toughness of life.
The huge heaviness in you
Made me lift every tough crisis –
And to hold, heaviness in the heart.

Everyone wishes to have you,
Your tempting sweetness and taste
But I also wish to taste,
Your pleasant luring aroma,
I love you to the inner core!!!
My Sweet love...Mr Jack!!!